Unlearning The World

Poems on Self, Society and Nature

Khirod C. Moharana

/ BookLeaf
Publishing
India | USA | UK

Made with ❤ on the BookLeaf Publishing Platform

www.bookleafpub.in

www.bookleafpub.com

Dedication

To those quiet rebels who dare to question
To those who refuse to accept the world as it was given
To those young people who are confused with endless
varieties of traditions
And to every soul who learned to see with their own
eyes

Preface

This book was born when I realised that unlearning is necessary for learning. The poems emerged at various moments of my life when unlearning was spontaneous and inevitable.

"Unlearning the World" recognises that individuals are not static; we persistently acquire new knowledge about humanity and the universe. Consequently, it is necessary to reassess and relinquish certain beliefs previously regarded as truths.

This book emerged from my ongoing internal struggle to understand human life and the universe. I realised that much of what we have learned over time no longer helps us perceive things as they truly are.

These poems promise to inspire us when knowledge itself becomes a veil.

I began to write these poems not as a poet, but as a witness — to what it means to live inside bodies, names, castes, genders, and truths handed down to us. I am here a witness to my learning and unlearning of what I understand as nature, society and self. From the very moment I open my eyes, I have been told who I am, what I may touch, what I must not desire, and what I must aspire to become.

But beneath all this conditioning lies something quiet and luminous — the self that still remembers how to be. *Unlearning the World* is my attempt to return to that remembering. It is a journey from belief to knowing, from acceptance to awareness.

These poems explore themes such as nature, society, self, consciousness, and various facets of human existence. The book further delves into faith, friendship, femininity, technology, liberation and hope. Each poem talks about learning new aspects and unlearning old beliefs. This book will take you to a path of personal awakening.

I write from within India's complex soil — where the sacred and the unjust often live side by side, where earth and divinity are both polluted and pure. Here, the poem must walk a double path: one of resistance, and one of reflection.

The book is an attempt to assert that our body is not impure for feeling. It strives to say that truth is not sacred because it is ancient but because it is alive.

If these poems speak at all, may they speak not of answers but of awakenings — of moments when the known begins to crumble and the real begins to breathe.

Acknowledgements

Writing Unlearning the World has been a long conversation with self, my parents, my wife and others who walked and questioned with me.

I am profoundly grateful to all the poets, philosophers, teachers, and friends whose voices have helped shape the language of reflection and resistance that these poems permeate.

I am deeply influenced by Mahatma Gandhi and B R Ambedkar who examined Indian society and hoped to bring changess. They continue to inspire even today and their courage is the unseen rhythm of these lines.

I am also indebted to my students whose questions about society and nature make me to think, rethink and sometimes change my presumptions. Their questions, sometimes innocent and sometimes political, keep my mind alive.

I am profoundly thankful to my friends, whose presence teaches that affection too is a form of liberation.

Finally, to those who believe that poetry can heal and awaken —

thank you for reading, for questioning, and for unlearning with me.

Khirod C Moharana

Prayagraj

1. No Other World

This is the World
That we see, live and remember
There is no other world
Except this land, water and space.
This is mundane
This is ordinary
This is our everyday.
Know it the way it is
No matter what they say
You see it
Live it
Experience it
All by yourself.
You see it yourself
Climb the hills
Cross the deserts
Dive into the bottom of the sea
All by yourself.
See the extraordinary
See the ubiquitous
See the sublime
All by yourself
And know

That they all are here
That there is no Otherworld.

2. Nature

A flower
Blossoms and shines
Attracts you and me
Entices honeybees
Plucked by man
Or dies of its own.
A river
Flows and descends
Gives lives
Makes civilizations
Swells and destroys
Changes course
Kills civilisations.
A deer
Runs and dances
Attracts you
And Sita
Eats tender leaves
And is eaten
By a lion.
Violent are they
And yet
There is no violence
Injustice as I see them

And yet
There is justice everywhere.

3. Society

I started my journey
With free upper limbs
Descended from the tree to the land
Ran for food and life
Killed and was killed
Asked my fellows to come together.
Searched for food
Succeeded
Failed and
Then I observed and learned
How to grow plants.
Got settled and made rules
Agreed to lessen my freedom
To live as a group
Made and lived with rules
Who lives with whom
Marries whom.
The older I became
The stronger became the group
I stopped to take birth
I was born into a group
Grew up, married as a member of a group
My death became a group affair
I stopped dying in solitude.

I ceased to think
To aspire, to realise
I was told
What to think, aspire and realise
I wasn't born
I was born into slots.
Now I am an animal
Tied to a peg
Designed by the group
No matter what they say
I do not exist
What exists is a society
Where dead men are born into slots.

4. The Big Question

We have come a long way
since we emerged on this planet
we crawled
stood and walked
ran...and killed
we ate and were eaten.
We have come a long way
We lived together
made families and groups
we made enemies
animals and men.
We have come a long way
we loved and hated
adored man and God
we waged war
worshipped nature
destroyed forest
killed animals
and we created
smoky sky and melting poles
new pathogens too
We have come a long way
Indeed, a long way...
but still ignorant

of who we are
and where we are !

5. Consciousness

Am I not the body?
The mind
Or the soul?
Am I not the one
Who is born into a slot of the society?
Am I someone bigger?
Perhaps the biggest?
Am I the King's son
-with no dearth of fulfilment
Armed with all weapons
in the battlefield?
When the battle will end
Will I get back again
to my own place?
-my own throne of thrones?

6. Sex

I was One
Wanted to become two
Divided my body into two
Two became four
Four became eight
The story continued
For a long time.
Nature wanted me to grow and change
I became bigger
A female me and a male me
Were born with an urge to mate
I became stronger
Could fight and live.
I was not satisfied
Didn't have hands, belly or head
It took a long time
Added all organs
Saw and heard the world
Ran, killed, and was killed
A male and a female
Sang again in the primal tone
I continued with new traits.

7. Caste

You are dumb
So is your father
So was your grandfather
All know that you are dumb.
Don't you believe
That you are dumb!
Are those dumb forefathers not enough
to say
That you are dumb!
Are your suppressed thoughts
And years of swallowed silence
not enough to say
That you are dumb!
You are dumb
Everyone says
You are dumb
Did anyone say
that you are the God?
Did anyone say
that you can think and speak?
You have been hearing this
You know this
That you are dumb.

8. Faith

Stormy midnight
Tormenting sky
Roaring sea
Swaying palms
Incessant rain
And the swinging nest.
His mother sings
Warm is her breast
He sleeps
He sleeps and dreams
Is this faith?

9. Memory

It was not autumn
A lonely leaf
Swayed to the ground
With music in the air.
The setting sun kissed
The red and purple flowers
With its golden ray
I smiled.
The sky whispered to me
in its dusky tone
the stars started blinking
The moon enticed me to its silvery path
I couldn't resist
Looked inside me
It was memory.

10. Femininity

I asked for two things
before coming to life
one that feeds
and the other that protects
One that loves and nurses
and the other that wins and proceeds
One that is feminine
and the other that is masculine.
Feminine taught me who I am
my band, my people
the forest, water, and the world
Listened to my vague words
My truth, my lies
my tales of triumph and defeat
taught me to win
to lose too.
Masculine with muscle and prowess
taught me to hunt for food
explore water
and to own land
to build houses and empire
to fight and conquere
It taught me to kill and rule
March ahead with bigul.

In my march in this world
I invented sword and wheel
Conquered groups and lands
worshpped masculinity
I forgot to nourish who nourished me
to love who loved me
I forgot to become weak
to lose and to become vulnerable
Forgot femininity.
Now I see the earth is dying
Ice melting
the planet warming
In my passion to win
I forgot to nourish
Me, my people and my planet.
The earth is dying
with smell of the End
Oh brother
enough of masculinity !
Lets us regain femininity
Let us nourish
that nourishes everything.

11. Hope

It is pitch dark,
And I am walking.
Since the last turn on my path,
I don't know
Where I am going.
Can you tell me
Where this road ends?
Where is it leading?
Can anyone say
How much dark is left
In my night?
Yet, I do not fear.
I will walk and pause,
Return and walk again—
Because I know:
The darkness will fade,
The sun will rise.

12. Darkness

Nothing I can see now
No road
no sky
no tree
no roadside houses,
I just feel
the earth on which
I am walking.
Don't know where I am going
where the road goes
Can feel the road edges
to straighten my journey
Don't know
what lies ahead
a nail or a flower
a dog or a snake
but I have to walk
by stumping my feet
by clearing my path
I have to walk
walk until I see
a little lamp
somewhere
far or near.

13. Friend

I want to talk—
to you.
I need to talk,
for each word I speak
makes me lighter.
So I found you,
my friend.
In talking,
I dive through layers of myself,
meeting the many faces
that live within me—
listening,
learning,
understanding.
I talk to you,
and in that sharing
something blossoms—
I grow,
I heal,
and you too
grow and heal
with me.

14. Nirvana

It is not dark
not light too
no desire
only being
it is that moment
I live here and now.
The wick is finished
no flames now
no past
no future
only the moment.
I can see
my body, my mind
the subtle movements
hear them...speak to them.
I can speak
to a flower, a tree, the sky
understand their words
look at their eyes
hug them
with free hands.
I am not my body
my mind nor my breath
but I am my source.

I am one
I am all.

15. Question, Don't believe

Question
Do not believe
Do not bow to what they say
Nor swallow what they prescribe
Question —
and know.
Unbind your mind
from borrowed truths
See with your own seeing,
know with your own knowing.
If belief you must hold,
know why you hold it
Trace the path of their knowing,
weigh their words
in the balance of your reason.
Let conviction, not obedience,
be your ground.
For there is no other way
To know is to taste
with the tongue of your own soul.
No voice can tell you
that a mango is sweet—
you must taste it to know.
I know the earth is round

because someone showed me
through eyes unclouded by faith,
through the clarity of method.
Question--
and know
and your soil will bloom,
your mind will grow green and fearless.
Innovation will rise
like dawn over your land,
and every heart
will become a spring of resource.

16. Self

I came into this world,
Drinking the warmth of my mother,
Saw her eyes — oceans of light,
Kissed her silence,
Spoke without words,
And from her love,
A part of me was born.
Then I saw the man —
The provider of dawn and shelter,
Who taught me sweat and sword,
Patience and pride;
In his strength and silence
He carved another part of me.
I grew beside him —
Played and fought,
Walked his paths,
Shared his bread,
And sometimes, his hunger too;
Together we built
Another part of me.
Then came love —
Fierce and tender,
Showing me what it means to be soft,
To see beauty in yielding;

She taught me femininity,
And shaped a subtle,
Sublime part in me.
I met the one
Who walked beside me
Through war and through victory,
Through sorrow and song,
In body, in mind —
And from that union
A joyous self emerged.
At last I met the one
To whom I spoke everything —
From sacred to profane,
From tenderness to wild laughter;
With words and silences
And the rest of my being was born.

17. Shudra

Why build temple?
whom to worship?
gods are everywhere
in you and in me,
don't buy their words
some are purer than the rest
because they have different blood?
Some are nearer to liberation
because of their birth?
You are Consciousness
eternal
free from the very beginning
see within
know your desire
your cravings
and know your self.
dont belive that you take birth
you have unlimited time
births and rebirths
you see yourself
and be yourself
that is samadhi
that is temple,
body takes birth

not the Consciousness
and you are the Consciousness
not the body
not a shudra as they say.

18. Label

They gave me my name
My surname
even before I came here
soft but resilient as a stone.
I met people
could hear that name
between the lines
and sometimes
on the lines,
I believed
And became that
I became a brahman
A kshyatriya, a vaishya
Or a shudra,
I didn't believe
And I became
A human being.

19. Liberation

See around
the cages, of gold and of iron
see them
witness them binding
and unbinding
and just see
that they were
your own illusion.
See the cages of knowledge
they tell you
to do this and avoid that
to kneel and
to perform rites
to be fearful and guilty,
Defy them all
You don't need fear
nor guilt
to exist,
and if they say
you need more births
to find the walls as air
to see the world as it is
Break the shackles
and declare that

I am you
not births away from you
I am free
here and now.

20. Technology

I once ran
for food and shelter,
a wanderer beneath an unknown sky.
I knew no fire,
no wheel —
only hunger and the wind.
Then I watched the forest breathe,
and learned from its secret sparks.
Fire was born —
a red flower of warmth and fear.
It guarded me,
fed me,
and I tasted the first cooked dream.
The wheel followed —
a turning of thought,
a circle of motion and time.
With watermills and pots,
I began to shape the world
as my own reflection.
I watched the soil,
sowed it with wonder —
agriculture grew,
and the bullock cart sang its slow song
toward the age of steam.

Through glass I peered —
the microscope revealed
a universe in a drop.
And I knew then
it was not gods or goddesses
who birthed disease,
but nature —
patterned, patient, profound.
Experiment became prayer,
observation, revelation.
I saw how the world worked,
and in knowing,
grew closer to truth.
Then came the machine —
and its dreaming child, the computer,
a mirror made of logic and light,
half human, half thought.
These are no tales of faith,
but of seeing, testing, knowing.
Not conjecture, not miracle,
but the long labor of reason.
Each invention,
a verse in the poem of empiricism —
each discovery,
a step away from fear.
For science is the fire
we still carry,

to keep the night of superstition
at bay.

21. Mirror

I wanted to see myself
all walls and corners of my being
all dresses of different colours
all moles and scars on my body
and I didn't succeed.
I invented friend
talked to him
loved, fought and cajole
together we won
lost too
but didn't succeed
in seeing
the entire me
in him.
Invented wife
shared food and shelter
aims and obligations
victories and frustrations
body and mind
sometimes happy
sometimes resentment
still
I couldn't get to see
how I look

after I peel off
all layers from my self.
I wanted to see
myself in full frame
in each space and moment
and I am still waiting.